Let the Marriage Begin!

A practical guide to getting married
and surviving your first year

Delores Hamilton

authorHOUSE®

DreamWorks Publishing, PLLC

AuthorHouse™
1663 Liberty Drive
Bloomington, IN 47403
www.authorhouse.com
Phone: 1-800-839-8640

Published by AuthorHouse & DreamWorks Publishing, PLLC 5/7/2012

ISBN: 978-1-4685-8803-3 (sc)
ISBN: 978-1-4685-8801-9 (hc)
ISBN: 978-1-4685-8802-6 (e)

Library of Congress Control Number: 2012906975

Editor: Catherine Frenzel
Cover Design: Jessica Busby

For information on Delores's services,

Call: 704-968-2253
Write: DreamWorks Publishing, PLLC
        2932 Breezewood Avenue, Suite 105
        Fayetteville, NC 28303
Email: Dreamworkspublishingpllc@gmail.com
Website: www.Dreamworkspublishingpllc.com
Follow her on Twitter at www.Twitter.com/DreamWorksPub

Many Thanks to All

I would like to dedicate this book to my parents, Tim Jackson and Judy Hamilton. They have given me the foundation of learning how to always improve in life by reviewing my part in the world and then regrouping. I want to let Anthony and Kenya know that I love them both very much. To Donna, Annette, Joyce, Lois, and Jeffrey for always being my sounding board, no matter what, and for always being able to tell me the truth and get me back on track. To my three sons, Stephan, Lance and Kendall, I love you all so very much! I pray that you all continue to strive to be the best men that you can be and have opportunities to enjoy the many blessings that life has to offer. I pray that you find happiness, health and prosperity. Special thanks to my cousins, Altamit, Trish and Ola, you ladies mean more to me than you will ever know, I am glad that you all are a part of my life. I couldn't have written this book without the help of my "sex and the city crew" – Latachia, Lynetta and Cynthia. You all are so bright and giving in your spirits and your husbands are very lucky to have you. To Marcella, Tammy, Shurray, Renee, Donna and Val – thank you for always being in my life as timeless friends.

There are so many wonderful people in my life to whom I want to give honorable mention, such as Carlos Todd, Ph.D.; William Humphrey, Tonia Allen, Toyia Reid, Robert Castle, Belinda Vaughters, Janice

Jeremy, Carol Bailey, Angie Traylor, Dellyne Samuels, Carroll Lytch, Psy.D.; Elizabeth Peterson-Vita, Ph.D.; Wendy Wellborne Kimery, Angel Green, Cherilyn Carter, Raquel Cox-Tennal, Linda Holeman-Block, Yvonne Ward, Dietrich Stewart and Pam Idol; the list could go on forever.

To all of the people in my life, please know that your friendship does not go unnoticed and that I appreciate you. To my editor, Catherine, you always have such a positive outlook and your motivating spirit allows me to keep me moving forward. To Christina, your ability to get a job done is so impressive; your work ethic and professionalism is amazing. I am so blessed to have you both on my team – or should I say as a part of my family!

I believe that in order to do well with being married, one must have examples to live by. So, to Yolanda and Roye, Karla and Tony, spending time with all of you has given me tools to be successful in my marriage and has allowed me to have an understanding of basic fundamental principles to share with other couples.

For the world is filled with doom and gloom, and there is something that should be said about people who are in love and stay in love, no matter what the obstacle; their love stands the tests of time. God bless everyone.

Contents

Forward

Having a baby is one of the greatest miracles a woman can experience. I wish there were a way one could bottle the experience. I absolutely loved being pregnant. Most importantly, I am blessed by the gift I was given of having a healthy pregnancy and having a healthy, beautiful, baby boy as a result of the process. When seeing a pregnant woman at a party or at a restaurant, I often look forward to having the conversation about what she is experiencing. I often ask questions like: What are you craving? Do you have Braxton-Hicks contractions? What is your favorite sleep position? Are you very tired most of the time? I can go on and on. The point is: After I had such a miraculous experience, I wanted to share the experience with everyone.

The same holds true for marriage. I believe that marriage is such a sacred, wonderful experience. So great, that some people can't wait to have the experience of being married. The experience of feeling as one with another person, having a confidant and a companion to share your life with is priceless. As a psychotherapist, I have spent a lot of time helping couples resolve their issues. Not to mention that I have spent many Girls' Nights out discussing the topic of marriage, especially marriage in the first year.

Over the years, I have discussed the intricacies that occur in the marriage experience so much – and found that people were being helped by what I had to say. I was led to write this book in order to share the information with as many people as possible, even with the whole world. I have come to learn that there are basic, fundamental dynamics that occur in the beginning of a marriage that, due to being so caught up with being in love, people do not expect to encounter and, therefore, fail to plan. Thus, once they are thrust into the midst of their marriage, issues arise, and the couple begins to feel all alone with what they are experiencing.

Well, you don't have to be frightened or embarrassed, or talk with relatives and friends who, although they love you, may not be able to help you allow your marriage to grow and prosper. Just relax. A solution to your problems is in your hands.

Know that you are not alone in your marriage, and yes, what you are experiencing is a normal process of loving and growing together. My hope for you is that you will feel vindicated by knowing that you had the courage to seek out answers to your current situation. They are right here at your fingertips by reading this book and getting prepared for what you are experiencing now and the issues that may arise in the future.

Let the Marriage Begin! can be used as a Marriage Manual by any individual who is interested in loving another and spending their life with that special person. It is designed to have you take an inward look at you, what you want, what you need to work on and how to work on your issues while learning to love another and grow with that person, all at one time.

Now, begin to read, begin to learn, begin to look into yourself and begin to truly love.

Namaste.

THE CHASE

Sierra and Roger met at a company Christmas party. She was the sister of his co-worker, Sienna. Sierra was often at the office going to lunch with her sister. Sierra, a free-lance writer, exuded a certain freedom that Roger admired. Roger was fortunate in life that when it came down to dating, he had so many opportunities to see women that he often had to turn dates away. However, Sierra did not notice Roger, ever. Even though Roger had his pick of any available woman in the room, he could not stop thinking about how he could get Sierra's attention. He had become enamored by her beauty, confidence and finesse.

While having lunch one day, Roger finally engaged Sierra in conversation that he hoped would lead to a very merry Christmas. It didn't. He left the restaurant puzzled that a woman could resist his charms. Thus, he proceeded to scroll through his Blackberry for the next best thing, anyone. Not the very merry Christmas he was hoping for.

At lunch several months later, Roger noticed the silhouette of someone enticing and familiar out of the corner of his eye. Sierra breezed past on her way to a booth. Roger made a bee line toward her as if he were expecting her as his lunch date. He asked if she was alone; she was. He invited her to join him, and the more conversation they had, the more he realized that his lifetime of superficiality with countless women could be *over. After exchanging numbers, and excited by the unique qualities that Sierra possessed, Roger was now in the midst of the thrill of the chase.*

Society has taught women to look forward to working, having a husband, beautiful children and a lovely home. The order of these requirements is not that important, but the preference for most women is: husband before children, having a successful career, a beautiful home and a nest egg to boot. Men, on the other hand, are taught that marriage should occur when the prime of their social adventuring is over. They have been given the message that obtaining a life partner is a deficit instead of an asset. "Have all the fun you can with all the women you can, while you can" is a message that has been implanted in the minds of many men.

No matter what messages are embedded in our subconscious mind, the need to be loved supersedes all notions of men constantly "playing the field." Seeking a committed relationship, despite the messages given by society, prevails. Hence, both men and women spend a great deal of their life seeking a mate with whom to share their life experiences. Some even believe in the notion that there is a kindred spirit to be found in another person somewhere in the world, and once the two spirits are joined together, the puzzle of love will have been completed. If one is ever lucky enough to experience a miraculous connection, it can speak to having a soul mate in life, and one should feel blessed.

You spend your time dating Mr. "He'll Do for Now," Mr. "He's Not the Marrying Type," or Ms. "Never That," and let's not forget Ms. "Oh Hell No!" So the dating goes on and on until you finally find Mr. or Ms. "Right." You begin to realize that this person meets whatever criteria you have developed to deem someone worthy to be a life partner. A word to the wise: If you don't have a checklist of what you are looking for, then you need to develop one, and ask yourself what are your non-negotiable, must-have qualities in a mate. The old adage states, "Those that stand for nothing fall for anything." So, create your standards and don't let standards be created for you by someone else when you're in the midst of a relationship.

The natural instinct for women during the thrill of the chase is to be caught. How one goes about ensuring that they are captured takes much planning and preparation. One must consider the following factors: What is the other person looking for in a mate? Can I meet the criteria of that person without major compromise of my own values? Does this person have my best interests at heart? Is this person reliable? Can I trust this person? And, are we spiritually, emotionally, physically and sexually compatible? These are questions you should consider when trying to get caught in the chase.

Conversely, a person can give you exactly what you are looking for, but only time will tell you if he or she is genuine. The thrill of the chase is successful only when you capture someone you believe is well-deserving of being chased; therefore, the challenge of being a worthy prize is paramount. One must be in a position of being independent, having clear value systems, willing to set boundaries, and be open and willing to have fun, to enjoy the art of the chase so as to get caught in the wonderful web of marriage.

By the way, although women traditionally like being caught, please note that in the world of equal opportunity, one caveat to consider is that women have mastered the thrill of the chase. So, when all is said and done, a young man may ask the question: Did I chase, or did I get caught?

Questions to ask yourself when you are in the midst of the chase. Take time now to answer the questions in this section.

1. What qualities are you looking for in a mate?

_____

_____

_____

_____

_____

2. What can you offer to a relationship?

_____

_____

_____

_____

3. What is your plan for a relationship, long- or short-term?

_____

_____

_____

_____

4. Is he or she worthy of being in a relationship with you? Why?

_____

_____

_____

_____

_____

5. What are your non-negotiable standards in a relationship?

_____

_____

_____

_____

_____

6. What qualities attracted you to the person that you are interested in?

_____

_____

_____

_____

_____

THE CATCH

Sammie and Crystal have been dating for 18 months. Sammie sat on a park bench evaluating his life. He thought about the blessings that have been bestowed upon him. Sammie has a great job; he has wonderful friends. He has a loving family and a beautiful home. As Sammie has spent all of his twenties and most of his thirties enjoying the fruits of his labor, he has begun to realize that he is ready to share his hopes and dreams, his fears and his heart with someone permanently. Crystal is the first person Sammie thinks of when he wakes up in the morning. Sammie reflects on what their children will look like.

Crystal has known for months now that Sammie is the person with whom she would love to grow old. They seem to share the same values about life, and Crystal knows he has her best interests at heart. Crystal often discusses with her friends the great, caring qualities that Sammie possesses that are so different from her previous relationships.

After pondering for hours about this major life decision, Sammie has prepared to set the stage to meet Crystal that night to ask for her hand in marriage.

So, you have finally met Mr. or Ms. Right, and the relationship is going well. You are tangled in the whimsical web of being in a serious relationship, which is exactly where you wanted to be. You have had opportunities to meet the family, learn many of his or her habits, and spend time together in many different settings. After considerable discussion, you have come to an amicable agreement on moral constructs such as religion and how you plan to worship, children, past relationships, pets, health issues, disagreements, sexual preferences, finances, where to live, purpose in life, deciding on your last name, and how to address future issues that you may encounter.

Without clearly understanding each person's frame of reference on the aforementioned fundamental topics, one will certainly be faced with conflict as issues arise in these areas. This is a great time in the relationship to have a discussion about various issues so that you learn more about the person with whom you are considering a long-term relationship. Despite being infatuated, take time out to be practical and discuss the following life issues.

RELIGION

Religion is a topic that one must discuss if you plan on having God, or whoever your spiritual guide may be, as a part of your marriage. The saying that "Marriage is a three-stranded cord that will survive only if God's third cord is present in the marriage" is a driving force for many people. You may come from different religious points of view. If so, you need to have a conversation about how you plan to worship – or not. You must decide how you will interact with your church family. Will both parties attend church regularly? Will you both be actively involved in church, such as going three times a week to attend bible study, regular church service and/or choir practice? Will you be able to come to terms with your spouse making the decision to not attend church at all while you believe it is your entire foundation for success as a couple?

When times get tough, and they will, a couple must be of one accord as to how they will handle the tough times. It will be the tough times that build your character as a couple, and having a foundation or a plan as to how you will confront hard times will be a key component to being prepared for whatever may come your way.

CHILDREN

Children are wonderful aspects of a relationship. A conversation should certainly occur to discuss whether or not each party would like to have children. And remember to discuss how many each of you would like to have. Is adoption an option? It is also important to discuss expectations of the role of the mother and father and the philosophy on how to raise children. Each individual comes from a different upbringing and brings to the table his or her own philosophy on how children should be raised, disciplined and educated.

Sometimes, a decision must be made about the willingness to marry a person who has children from a previous relationship. If one is willing to be in a relationship with step-children, then the discussion of how the relationship can be successful with a blended family must occur. It can be done, but roles must be clear.

With blended families, be prepared to have a relationship with the other parent, since all of you are now responsible to raise the children to be healthy, nurturing adults. Some of these major discussions should include:

- How to develop a relationship with the birth mother or father when making family decisions about the children
- Continuously working on relationship-building with your spouse and the other parent so that there can be an amicable understanding
- How does discipline occur with the step-children?
- Most importantly, how your spouse interacts with his or her previous partner will determine the energy of your

relationship. Will either of you carry the luggage of the old relationship into the new one?

Bringing emotional baggage from an old relationship happens on a regular basis for many people (see below), and the world wonders why the divorce rate is so high. Will you hold onto your ex as a dear friend that you must stay in contact with? Will you allow yourself to be free from the past to embark on your future? It must be mentioned again that when children are involved, you are in a relationship with the other parent, like it or not. Conversations along with clear boundaries must occur in order to be successful in these blended relationships.

PAST RELATIONSHIPS

What old baggage are you carrying? Past relationships, if they go unresolved, have a way of creeping into your current situation. As you are moving toward developing a new relationship, a conversation will need to occur around past associations, how they ended, if there has been closure on the relationship for both parties, and have you allowed yourself time to heal from the previous breakup. While you are trying to develop a union with the new person in your life, explore these issues, and make sure the baggage has been left at another terminal before you move forward. You may have heard many horror stories of marriages ending prematurely due to extramarital affairs with the previous partner. These occur, in part, due to the lack of closure in that relationship – so, beware, and discuss this issue.

PETS

Pets are like children for many people. The relationship one has with their pet is developed over time and is very special. Have you discussed the option of having pets in your home? Have you discussed what type of pets, how many, and what is the maximum number of pets you are willing to have? Will your pets live in or outside of your home? Will they be allowed on the furniture or not? How will you compromise if your spouse doesn't care for pets? There are many people who have no emotional connection to pets and don't want pets to be a part of their lives. Can you handle being a person that loves pets and your mate doesn't? Talk about it and come up with a happy medium if you can. If you cannot decide on a middle ground in this arena, you may need to decide to go your separate ways now.

DISAGREEMENTS

It is paramount that you have an idea of how each person will deal with conflict and disagreements. You will want to know how your partner will react when he or she becomes upset with you.

As a woman, you will tend to discuss your issues with your friends when you are upset with your spouse. I can tell you that if a situation is not a physically or emotionally abusive, you will need to come up with creative ways to deal with being momentarily upset without harming your partner's ego in the long-run. I have always been a proponent for removing oneself from the situation to allow some time to think clearly before saying or doing something that you may regret. For example, leaving your home and going to a public place like Wal-Mart, which is open at all hours and has plenty of traffic, where you can breeze through the shopping aisles, will allow you to calm down and relax.

A word of caution: Be very careful when leaving your home upset because it can be very dangerous if you are not cognizant of your surroundings because your emotions are out of control. You will also need to come up with ways in which you can redirect your anger and frustration and get to a point where you can resolve any of your disagreements in a calm manner.

Men appear to avoid confrontation like the plague. Having disagreements is just uncomfortable, so, at all costs, no matter what, they will try their best not to deal with issues they feel are causing conflict and confrontation. The biggest communication tool/secret I can ever give you is to have you understand that men are typically dominant in their left brain, which is more focused on logic, details and strategy. This is why men see issues only in black and white with not much grey. It will take them a considerable amount of time to deal with issues by allowing their thoughts and the issue at hand to be processed by the right brain, which consists of emotions, appreciation and possibilities. So, women, lay the issue on the table, give them about one hour or so to process, and ask them to come back to you to discuss the issue. Most men can do this.

But there is a possibility that the man can be so shut-down emotionally that he will not want to deal with any issues; then, you have a different issue of emotional isolation that you must decide how to deal with. Always remember that women are designed to address issues immediately so that they can relieve their stress levels by getting some type of emotional resolution. The old adage that "men are from Mars and women are from Venus" highlights the differences in emotional processing between men and women. Once each individual realizes that each person will process emotions, logic, issues and disagreements differently, you have a better chance of success at resolving conflict within your relationship with each other.

SEXUAL PREFERENCES

My personal opinion is that what goes on in one's bedroom is strictly their business. At this phase in your relationship, you may have already consummated your union. Of course, the Bible indicates that the sacred act of sex should not occur until after you have become officially married, but you have to choose that path on your own. Whenever you get to the phase in your relationship where sex is being considered, you must have a conversation about your preferences regarding sexual matters. In today's society, there has been a disintegration of values regarding sex, so – unless casual sex is your thing and you are willing to have sex on the first or second date – you need to know as much as you can about the person with whom you are planning on being intimate.

If you want to know about previous relationships that your partner has had, talk about it. Some individuals prefer not to know about who and how many people the potential partner has been with before, and want to move forward regardless of the past. The bottom line here is, you have to decide your position on past relationships and be prepared to move forward.

The other major discussion you need have is about your partner having sex with someone of the same sex. In other words, has your partner been or are they now on the "down low," which means not exposing their choice to have sex with people of the same gender? How you do feel about their preference? And how do you feel about their cover-up?

Swinging is another issue that couples must discuss because some people are all for "open relationships" and having sex with other couples. If you are not having a completely monogamous relationship, you will need to know if your partner is on the same page.

In these current days of HIV/AIDS being so rampant, conversations about these topics must happen because knowledge is power, and you want to have the power to keep your body clear and free of disease. So, talk about it before jumping in bed with your partner so that you know what you are getting. Remember, one night of pleasure can lead to a lifetime of pain; but if you are honest and have had the tough discussions, the night of pleasure can lead to many, many more.

HEALTH ISSUES

On the matter of health issues, have you and your new mate discussed the possibility of either of you having a lifelong illness, and how you would handle those situations? What about if either of you were in a position where you could not speak for yourself. Would your mate be able to handle your affairs and would he or she know how you would like for them to be handled? So often, we think we have time to plan for the future; well, you are currently and fortunately in the planning stages right now. So talk about this issue now.

As you are preparing for your blessed union, you also need to talk about how to prepare for the unthinkable. For example, once you become a unit, and as a couple, you live in a city different from your parents, what type of funeral preparations will need to occur for you and your spouse. Funeral arrangements and agreements may need to be discussed for your parents as well. These are issues we don't like to think about, but trust me, if we do not think about them, inevitably, when the time arises, you are forced to think about it and make decisions on the spot. It would make a difficult time a bit easier if preplanning had occurred surrounding this topic. And remember to treat each day as a present. Always work at cherishing the time you have together.

FINANCES

Money is a factor that should be reviewed prior to getting to this stage of planning. Before popping the question and asking another person to be your life partner, you want to have knowledge of their credit score and any outstanding debts they possess. You need to know about each other's spending and saving habits. Conversations should have already taken place about each person's financial portfolio and how you plan on merging the two. Pre-marital financial planning would be a great way to start.

Today, it has become common to hear couples develop prenuptial agreements. With the divorce rate being so high, and the divorce laws trying to protect spouses to ensure they can still survive, people are trying to have a security blanket for the wealth they bring to the table. This issue is controversial for many reasons, so discuss it and know where you stand as a couple regarding this topic.

From listening to Steve Harvey on the radio, as well as talking with many of my friends, I have been fortunate enough to have received the best advice. The best way to have a basic workable financial structure as a couple is to:

- Have one savings account that money is placed into, but never touched. This account should require two signatures in order to make a withdrawal. Remember, this is the money that should grow.
- There should be another account for each individual where you have money for your own personal shopping and purchases.
- You should have one checking account from which all of the bills are paid.
- And, for those of you who take advice from your elders, you should always have a "rainy day fund" just in case your relationship doesn't work out.

Now, I must tell you that I am on the fence with the last "just in case" account. I understand the premise of the account. On one hand, it is just like the safety net of the prenuptial agreement. On the other hand, it speaks to the lack of trust that you have in your relationship and it could set you up for a self-fulfilling prophecy if you have an exit or get-out-of-the-marriage plan. I believe you should spend some serious time thinking about this type of account and come up with your own conclusions.

- Finally, you should secure Roth and Simple IRAs, CDs and/or mutual funds to allow your money to continue to grow for you and your spouse.

This is a basic financial structure to give you the stepping stones for success. You will need to discuss how bills will be paid, how each person will have the opportunity to spend money, etc. You may also want to discuss how you plan on building or keeping your wealth. Financial situations can often change, so having conversations about financial emergencies and how to handle them will be important.

Also, our society has become so comfortable with having two-income households and using all of the income to survive. Based on our current economical state, it would be wise to begin your new life living on one salary if possible and using the other for a rainy day, as they are sure to come. Word to the wise: Do not get caught up in trying to keep up with the Joneses. If I am not mistaken, they lost their home in foreclosure for living beyond their means.

WHERE TO LIVE

Here are some issues you will need to explore when considering where to live. Will you live in the same location as your parents? Will you live in a city away from family? Will you live in the city, or would you prefer living a suburban lifestyle? In essence, you will you need to discuss geographic location. For some people, living arrangements may not be an issue; that is great. For others, geographic location can pose many problems now or in the future. For example, if you live in a city away from family, and you have no family support, it can be lonely and cause much expense and travel if you are really close-knit with your family. Another issue is the opposite: When you live near your family and they are visiting so often, it can become intrusive to your marriage (depending on the relationship you have with the family and in-laws).

As for home ownership, have you made a decision what to do if both parties are homeowners prior to getting married? Who places their home for sale? Do you sell both homes and buy a new home together? Have you discussed what type of home you want to have? And if you choose to purchase a home, have you come to a conclusion about how much you can afford to spend? There are many situations to discuss regarding where you will live, so start talking about them now.

PURPOSE IN LIFE

Do you have purpose? What is your blueprint in life as a couple? Have you decided what your mission and vision statement will be as a couple? Have you discussed where you plan on being as a couple in one, five, and even fifty years from now? The reality of your newfound loving relationship is the fact that you are in your infancy stage, or one could say the infatuation stage. Hence, the intensity of the relationship and the ecstasy of loving each other could get in the way of thinking ahead.

Talk about your mission, vision and purpose as if you are developing a business. You are designing a foundation that will carry you through the rest of your life. Please note that the blueprint can and will be redefined as time goes forward, but you need to at least have one to begin with so you know where you are going. Consider this discussion to be your navigation system (GPS) to where you are trying to go in life.

An example of a purpose statement for your relationship could be as simple as this:

*As a couple, we will strive to improve ourselves
individually in an effort to grow together.*

Your mission could be:

To love each other unconditionally

Your vision is what your life will look like in the future if you follow your mission and purpose, so, as a couple, your vision could be:

To live healthy, prosperous lives by keeping our

> *spirituality in the forefront of our life while*
> *allowing each person to grow individually.*

When times get tough, and they will, and you seem to get off track, you should always be able to go back to your mission, vision and purpose statements to assist you in remembering why you decided to join as a union to begin with. These guiding principles are your glue, your roadmap when times get tough. So, develop them now, and you will be glad you did later.

DECIDING ON YOUR LAST NAME

Another area of planning is for the couple to decide on how the last name of the husband will be attached to the wife. Historically, based on women wanting to outwardly express their new union, she would take the surname of the husband. As women have become more independent and powerful in the corporate world, it has become more important for the woman to keep her individuality, thus keeping her own surname. In an effort to have the best of both worlds, women have adopted hyphenated last names.

Also to be considered, which surname will go first? For example, some cultures believe in having the maternal surname precede the paternal surname. Have this conversation ahead of time, so that you know what you will be called from here on out.

In the future, the last name of your children will be a factor as well. What will your last name mean for you and your children?

FUTURE ISSUES

There are many situations and issues that may arise that one or both of you will not anticipate happening. You will need to have the skills, no matter what the issue, about how to address unforeseen events. There are some things in life that are certain, such as death and taxes. In our lives, we will deal perhaps with illness, financial misfortune, career transition, having an in-law move in, winning the lottery, etc. You will need to have a plan on how to address such future issues. It is a good time now, in the preparation process, to discuss how you plan on dealing with such possible circumstances. Have a conversation about such things as having either of your parents come to live with you and you becoming their caretaker. Are either of you prepared to make that adjustment and still function as a couple?

I know it is difficult to discuss how you address issues that have not occurred yet. You actually have no idea how you will feel about some of the future issues that may arise. The point of having a conversation – now – about future issues is to learn as much about one another as you possibly can. This subject is giving you an opportunity to increase communication and begin discussing life areas that can cause future discord in marriages. By discussing these issues in advance, you will be ahead the game, and happy that you had the foresight to talk about these areas and to have a notion of where each of you stand if and when some of these issues arise in your future union.

Questions to ask yourself when you are in the midst of being caught. Take time to answer the questions in this section.

1. What is it about this person that stands apart from anyone else?

_____

_____

_____

_____

_____

2. What factors have contributed to your decision to be in a committed relationship?

_____

_____

_____

_____

_____

3. Why is this relationship different from any other?

_____

_____

_____

_____

_____

4. What are your mission, vision and purpose statements for this
   relationship?

   _____

   _____

   _____

   _____

   _____

5. Is it the particular person or the act of being in a relationship that
   has you in this relationship? Why?

   _____

   _____

   _____

   _____

   _____

6. What life areas do you think will need intensive discussion as a
   couple?

   _____

   _____

   _____

   _____

   _____

THE CHAOS OF PLANNING

Blake and Victoria were excited about coming together as one. Blake lost both his parents at an early age. Victoria grew up in a single-parent home, and her mother could not afford to pay for a dream wedding as Victoria would have hoped. Nonetheless, the wedding must go on, so Blake and Victoria decided to develop a budget and fund their wedding.

Where to begin? First, they must have an engagement party to announce to the world that they are officially coming together as one. They have decided on a budget for a glorious wedding that will be the talk of the town for years to come. They will have to plan on how many people they want in their wedding party, how many guests to invite, what to wear, what venue will suffice, who will officiate, what to eat, how to decorate, how to celebrate, where to go for the honeymoon, how to combine their lives as one. In the midst of deciding to become one, the couple is now engulfed in the chaos of planning.

As a couple, you should already have discussed major life issues and how to handle problems together. You have a strong sense of knowing that you plan on growing old with this person, and now are about to embark on what is usually a stressful time in your life where you must plan and execute the details of coming together as one. This is an exciting and scary time for both parties. Women get to tell all of their friends they are off the market, and begin immediately with wedding planning. Men get to hear how their lives are over as they know it. Fortunately, love prevails, and they ignore this type of negative banter from their friends who are either comfortable with the single lifestyle or jaded because of love gone wrong and really don't want to see another man go down the road of heartache or successful marital bliss.

Traditionally, the family of the bride has the honor of paying for the wedding ceremony and giving the bride to the groom in preparation for him to now take care of her for the rest of her life. For those of you who are blessed with having this opportunity of tradition, congratulations! For the rest of the world that will end up paying for this grand event out of your own pocket, be prepared to spend, spend and spend.

If you are financially savvy, then making a budget and sticking to it to celebrate your magical union will be to your advantage as you enter into your new world as a couple. Often, the fairytale gets in the way of the reality, and many people end up in the poor house in an effort to celebrate their union with family, friends and acquaintances. Thanks to the wonderful world of reality television, people can now advertise their sense of entitlement to having a fairytale, no matter what the cost.

So, what exactly are you planning? Let's see: One has to plan for the location of the blessed union, the location for the celebration of the union (the reception), where you will go to honeymoon after your union, and of course, where you will live after you have been united. This could be as simplistic or complicated as one would choose to make it. Let's also remember: what to wear, who to invite, who will be in the wedding party, who will sing, who will take photos, who will cater, who will DJ, who will officiate; what type of flowers, lighting, transportation, and other elaborate arrangements you will have. The best-case scenario would be to have a trusted wedding planner coordinate all of these intricacies for you in an effort to assist you with sticking to a budget and minimizing your stress.

Now that the planning is underway, prepare for the stressors of pulling everything together and having possibly your first experience with dealing with multiple stressors at one time. Just because getting married is a positive event does not mean that you will not experience eustress (positive stress) and distress (negative stress) in the process. This is a great time for you to begin to develop an understanding of how to cope with future stressors in your life. Trust me – you're going to need the skills! You will need to learn to channel your stress now, so that you will be able to manage stress from here on out. Some of the ways in which you can reduce and manage your stress during this busy time in your life is to participate in an exercise program, listen to relaxing music, meditate, get a massage if it is in the budget, telephone a friend, dance, and – most of all – have fun and enjoy life.

In the process of planning, there is the rite of passage that ends the culmination of being single. The bachelor and bachelorette party is your last hoorah for the life that you used to have and a celebration to welcome you to the new life awaiting you.

One day, you will realize that you're at the end of all the chaos of planning phase. During this final period of planning, it will be important to stay in the present while you are making arrangements for your big day. Keep in mind why you have decided to marry this person to begin with. Your motive for marriage will begin to manifest itself during the planning stages of pulling it all together. For example, if you are getting married because all of your friends are married, the planning of the wedding will be centered around who will be there to witness this event. There is, of course, the person that is marrying for love and the most important aspect of the marriage is obtaining a harmonious bond with your new mate.

In the midst of all of the wedding planning, it is important to plan on gaining knowledge, skills and tools to be successful in your new union. Pre-marital counseling allows you to begin to think through and process issues that, in the midst of your euphoria, you may not initially consider. Pre-marital counseling is the one of the best planning pieces for the marriage to have. Having foresight about dealing with common issues married couples experience is absolutely priceless!

Questions to ask yourself when you are in the process of planning. Take time to answer the questions in this section.

1. What does becoming a union with another person mean to you?

_____

_____

_____

_____

_____

2. What does the wedding mean to you?

_____

_____

_____

_____

_____

3. What is your primary goal for marriage, and are you staying on task?

_____

_____

_____

_____

_____

4. What obstacles have gotten in your way in the planning process, and how did or do you overcome them?

_____

_____

_____

_____

_____

5. What is most important to you during this planning process?

_____

_____

_____

_____

_____

6. Discuss your plan for premarital counseling.

_____

_____

_____

_____

_____

THE EVENT

Monica and Jim have spent eighteen months preparing for this day. There were many occasions when they thought they should call it quits because planning this big event was so stressful that it didn't seem worth the trouble.

As Jim finally watches Monica walk down the aisle, a tear streams down his cheek. He is the proudest man in the world. Once Monica stands next to Jim, the reverend begins discussing the importance of becoming a unit. He talks to the couple about what guiding principles they should follow. The couple exchanges their own vows to show their level of commitment to each other. They both express how they are committing themselves to the other by law and in the eyes of the Lord. They pledge their undying love toward one another; they discuss their promise to be faithful to one another and to let no issues tear them apart. They are then blessed by the church, pronounced husband and wife and proceed down the aisle as one.

All of the wedding planning has paid off. Everyone is dressed and ready for the big event. What type of union will you have? Will it be a civil union where you join in a contractual agreement honored by the state for the purpose of the distribution of property? Or, will you have a union that is a contractual agreement with a permanent promise in which your higher power is the center? You make the decision. The minister or whoever officiates covers the basic principles that are meant to be the foundation to your beginning and everlasting marriage. Some of the key principles that are discussed are the famous, "for richer or poorer, in sickness and in health and only in death do we part." If these words were honored in all marriages, then I am willing to bet that the divorce rate would not be at an ever-increasing 40% or more.

The ceremonial unionization of the couple has been complete. Now, all your friends and family have the pleasure of celebrating the coming together of the new Mr. and Mrs. "I am so happy I am married now!" After an exhausting and hopefully exhilarating night of celebrating, and collecting gifts, the lovely couple are off to consummate their coming together with an experience that should be so special and earth shattering, it should be a beautiful night to remember. Now the couple is off to enjoy the honeymoon, and then, the rest of their lives together.

The concept of the honeymoon in a marriage is to allot a time to love each other and relax as much as you can before having to go back to the real world and deal with the hustle and bustle of your reality. The word *honeymoon*, as it relates to marriage, describes this phase of the relationship as the "fantasy period," the time of your life where you don't argue with one another; you are in synch in every possible way. This stage is not meant to last, but enjoy it while you can. It is meant to be short, and all parties involved will be on their best behavior. Behold, the real world is coming to greet you soon with all of its joys, issues, challenges, and newfound realities. So, savor the honeymoon period of your marriage.

Questions to ask yourself when you are preparing for your big day. Take time to answer the questions in this section.

1. What was your emotional journey like during the actual wedding event?

_____

_____

_____

_____

_____

2. What did the experience of planning for this event teach you?

_____

_____

_____

_____

3. How have you grown as a couple during the planning process?

_____

_____

_____

_____

4. What will the role of a husband or a wife mean to and for you?

_____

_____

_____

_____

_____

5. What are your personal vows to your new spouse?

_____

_____

_____

_____

_____

6. What are your expectations of your new spouse moving forward?

_____

_____

_____

_____

_____

THE UNION

Richard and Marlene were so excited to finally live as husband and wife. They have been back from their honeymoon for three months now. As they begin to settle into daily routines and spend more time together, they begin to realize that being together and working through basic issues is getting to be a great deal of work. Even so, they are very happy with being together and are still thrilled about being united. But they hadn't planned on asking themselves, what in the world is going on with my new partner?

You are now in a position to proudly enjoy being a husband or being a wife. You have your wedding rings as an outward representation to show your never-ending commitment and mutual fidelity to one another and to the world. The essence of getting to know each other on another level is a blessing, and you officially have permission to begin doing so.

You get to wake up with your best friend every day. You are, based on the Good Book, able to have the best guilt-free sex as often as you like. You get to enjoy and explore each other as often as you can, and have someone to share your hopes, dreams and fears with unconditional regard. Having a monogamous relationship where you worship, vacation, dine, and spend quiet time together will make you feel as if you are the luckiest person in the world.

This beginning phase of being together is a great phase of marriage! These feelings and experiences are what you hold onto when you need to be reminded of why you married your soul mate. The honeymoon period is about loving, respecting, and cherishing one another. Hold onto to these memories because as the honeymoon period begins to wane, you enter a new realm of marriage that lends itself to you spending time scratching your head trying to figure out who this person is that you married and what happened to your dream mate.

This is not uncommon. What is happening is that each party is letting their guard down and is allowing themselves to become comfortable within the union to truly be themselves, with no holds barred. Each person tries to figure out how to keep the same level of passion and newness because it feels so good, but the energy must change as the dynamics of the marriage are changing.

As one becomes comfortable within their surroundings, it is natural to begin to let themselves get very comfortable in their skin. There is a sense of "finalizing the deal" when getting married and a sense of having won the prize, and this means the "true person" in "you" can now emerge. Don't get me wrong. I am not saying that a person changes completely. But what happens is that slowly and surely, the true values and opinions of the individual begin to emerge and they may not always be congruent to what the other party would like to hear or see. Thus, conflict begins to come into play, and each party begins to question the past conversations, current intent, and their partner's level of honesty.

Once an individual has been placed on alert regarding a change in personality, values and beliefs, a certain defensiveness occurs that places him or her in protective mode. There is a dichotomy between "I need to protect myself from whatever may come" and the sense of loving your spouse so much that you would do anything for that person. You are beginning to learn that there is a tug of war, an intricate set of movements occurring that form a dance. A dance that you are not familiar with, but a dance that you are forced to participate in as it is now guiding your life. It is the art of the dance that is taking place. So, let the dance begin!

Questions to ask yourself after you have spent some time with your new spouse. Take time to answer the questions in this section.

1. What are your expectations of each other as the novelty of being married fades away?

_____

_____

_____

_____

2. Having realized that you must do things differently now that you are married, what do you have to change?

_____

_____

_____

_____

3. What have you learned about respecting one another?

_____

_____

_____

_____

4. What are your plans for enjoying each other?

_____

_____

_____

_____

_____

5. What makes your communication work with each other – or not?

_____

_____

_____

_____

_____

6. What roles have been defined for each of you in your relationship?

_____

_____

_____

_____

_____

THE ART OF THE DANCE

When professional ballroom dancers perform, they are so mesmerizing and spectacular in their movement because of being in unison, and simultaneously forcing each other apart. The compelling beauty of the dance is created by how the dancers choose to come back together.

Stanley and Audrey have been married for eight months. Stanley is telling his friends that he believes he made a mistake in getting married because he didn't realize it would be so hard. Audrey is spending most of her days telling her friends that she married an imposter, and doesn't understand how Stanley could be so insensitive and uncooperative in the marriage. Despite the two talking to their friends to get advice, they are both feeling all alone during this time as they do not understand the fundamentals of the dance.

There is a certain beauty and sensuality in ballroom dancing. The intricacies and level of difficulty of the individual movements that work so well independently and allow you to come together and move fluidly as one are some of the most powerful, sensual illustrations of how this next phase in your first year of marriage will unfold. Once you have become unified, and the honeymoon period is over, the natural order of progression is to find out how to move together in one accord while keeping your individuality, independence and family plan intact.

The problem with the dance is that the small disagreements take you back to your level of comfort in dealing with conflict like you did when you were single. Being single, you didn't have to be accountable for and to others. You didn't get angry and have to stay in the home and deal with the person you were angry with. Being single, you always had the option to leave.

Each person should have come into the marriage with the understanding that compromise is necessary. It is necessary in order for a woman and a man to blend together in the midst of a spin while dancing in order to stay uniform and appear as one. It is necessary in order to keep the peace in your home. But how does one compromise without losing a piece of who they are in the process?

Well, in an effort to complete the dance, each partner must be committed to the flow and understand that compromise is a part of the rules. The dancers need an understanding of the extreme amount of vulnerability and trust in the unknown in order to be fluid and successful. It's about trusting the process and the purpose. It's about having faith and also remembering that winning the battle does not mean winning the war. It's not about always being right, it's not about what you used to do and how life was for you prior to this new era. You were in a different dance then, and you could master that dance all alone. There was no dance partner needed for you to be fabulous.

You are now required to learn how to follow in order to know how to lead. You must know when to compromise and when to praise. You must learn that in the midst of your ballroom dancing, the wall-to-wall mirror you are looking in is pointing at you and exposing your flaws. The mirror is designed to give you the opportunity to look at the exposed character defects in yourself and your partner, and to ask yourself if you can work on your issues individually. Simultaneously, you will still need to come together with your partner and be able to accept his or her personality flaws.

If you can master the art of looking at yourself in the mirror, acknowledge your issues, work on your shortcomings, and be OK with your partner having issues, giving him or her opportunity to work on their baggage also, brava and bravo!!! You have mastered the art of the dance, and you deserve a standing ovation.

This dance can also end many relationships because the issues that are viewed in the mirror are often reflected onto the other person, and then the dance is out of balance; each partner blames the other for their shortcomings, and the dance turns into a brawl. Regret sets in and the wonderment of "How did I end up here with this person?" is the ultimate thought process.

When the dance is not in step, the couple finds it very difficult to move on. Where would you go from here?

One road that will lead to disaster is, going to your family and friends to discuss your issues, concerns or discontent. The people in your life want the best for you, so when they believe that you are being harmed by your significant other, whether it is physically or emotionally, they take your side and make a personal pledge not to care for your spouse any longer. This certainly can be problematic as you begin to decide which road you would like to take.

The choices you make during the infancy stage of your marriage will carry into your future. If you need assistance with your dance, then choose a non-biased professional to help with your flow. It will help you in the long run to be more successful with your Tango, Fox Trot and Rumba. Enjoy the dance!

Questions to ask yourself when you are in the midst of the dance. Take time to answer the questions in this section.

1. What has changed in your relationship?

_____

_____

_____

_____

_____

2. When you are in conflict, what role do you play?

_____

_____

_____

_____

_____

3. Have you come to terms with adapting to new coping skills since you are no longer single? If so, what are they? If not, what do you need to change?

_____

_____

_____

_____

_____

4. Can you compromise? If so, what does it mean for you to compromise?

_____

_____

_____

_____

_____

5. What old baggage is standing in your way that could be causing friction in your relationship?

_____

_____

_____

_____

_____

6. What issues of yours are you now compelled to address?

_____

_____

_____

_____

_____

THE Y IN THE ROAD

Anthony and Carmen were barely speaking to each other. Nine months into their marriage; they were having serious discussions about calling it quits. Anthony believed that Carmen showed no respect toward him and Carmen believed that Anthony did not believe in her. Both parties had argued about their issues on numerous occasions, to no avail. Today, they decided to sit down and discuss where they go from here as a couple.

When you decided to take a vacation, you packed your bags, ensured you had enough money, loaded your car, filled the car with gas and began driving. But somewhere in the midst of planning your vacation, you forgot to decide on a destination. Well, here you are now: You have driven for hours with no destination in mind, and lo and behold, you are here at the unavoidable Y in the road. You have to make a choice. What will it be?

In first year of the marriage, each couple is destined to come to this inevitable place as issues begin to arise and go unresolved. You end up at the Y because you have come to a point in the relationship where one direction means that you have not come to terms with your own issues and you then redirect your angst onto your partner and magnify his or her flaws to make you feel better. The other direction means you have

49

dealt with your issues and allowed your partner to address theirs and decided to stay on the journey together.

Each individual may say to themselves at one point or another in the beginning of the relationship, "I should have stayed single. Life was much easier being single." And maybe it was. But life as a single person was so much easier because you were not dancing in the mirror at all or consistently enough for you to see your deficiencies, nor did you have another person so close to you to be there and expose your idiosyncrasies in a manner that forces you to be uncomfortable enough to have to address them. If you decide not to address your issues, and your partner is insisting upon a change to improve your relationship, then all defenses rise up and you, and maybe even your partner, get into a self-preservation mode of protecting yourself at all costs, and at the expense of growing further apart from each other.

Earlier, in the Chaos of Planning chapter, I talked about pre-marital counseling. This is an essential investment during the planning period of getting married. It is equally, if not more imperative, to have post-marital counseling to assist you as a couple in dealing with these new-found issues that other couples really don't talk about. Although people do not talk about their issues, the issues still exist. How else could two people get together under one roof and truly unify without working through situations and concerns?

Counseling is crucial at this Y-in-the-road phase of your relationship because you will have many tough decisions to make as to a clear direction to take. It will be advantageous for you to have some unbiased, professional assistance to help you sort through all you are experiencing in the midst of choosing a direction.

Experience has taught me that couples get into relationships and have no idea to what magnitude of issues the marriage itself forces you to address. Issues that you never thought you would have to attend to, or issues that you didn't know you had, now have to be confronted and resolved. Then, throw in the same situation for your spouse, and both of you are in the same boat. Mutual self-examination and hard work on finding resolution individually is the key to trying to being together as a couple.

Counseling will assist in deciphering your issues in this phase, but note that each person will have their own motivation to change – or not – at different times during this process, which also complicates the relationship. Much intervention is needed during this phase of your marriage, but ensure that you are getting the information from a place that won't hurt you or your partner in the long run. It is imperative that you are not discussing your personal relationship issues with family and friends. This time in your life is critical for building a foundation together. You would not want your foundation to be rattled by broken relationships with family members because of information you shared about your spouse that was bothering you at the time, and you have since moved on from the issue, and now your family or friends have placed a negative judgment on your spouse that will not go away.

The Y in the road allows you to have choices, even when you believe that there aren't any options regarding your situation. Oftentimes, when people are newly married and begin having relationship problems, the choices that are on the table are staying in the marriage and working it out, or severing ties and moving on individually. When making a life-altering decision such as this, each of you must stay in the mirror to soul search and be willing to be vulnerable and honest. You must be mindful of the fact that although you believe that your partner is causing all of the problems, you do have some part to play in the situation.

In order to decide on a road to take, you have to decide where you want to go and why you want to go there. Working on your issues will help you to determine which road to take. So, here you are at the intersection of indecisiveness. Before you make a decision to choose a road, I am going to ask you to take a detour and travel as a couple to any divorce court session. This will be one of the best adventures for your marriage. You can go any day of the week and sit in divorce court and listen to the hearings. One day of having this experience will also give you fuel for your decision-making as you are choosing a road. The road to divorce is one of the options, so you are fortunate to get a quick preview of what's on that road by sitting in on some of the divorce hearings to find out what that road can offer.

When you are at this intersection of life, you must choose wisely because each road has a destination, and you must be willing to take the journey that the road will place you on, once the choice is made. Please note that there is no right or wrong road. However, you will need foresight to know what to expect on the journey of the road that you choose. Once your decision is made, you must also be willing to follow through with your choice. The road that you choose is often a one-way street, so, in short, there is no turning back. You will need to choose wisely.

Questions to ask yourself when you are at the Y in the road. Take time to answer the questions in this section.

1. What tools have you tried to work out issues with your spouse?

_____

_____

_____

_____

_____

2. What are the core issues you are dealing with?

_____

_____

_____

_____

_____

3. What are your options if you are not willing to stay in your marriage?

_____

_____

_____

_____

_____

4. What vows or commitments did you make to each other?

_____

_____

_____

_____

_____

5. What will you gain if you walk away from your marriage?

_____

_____

_____

_____

_____

6. What will you gain if you decide to stay in your marriage?

_____

_____

_____

_____

_____

DIVIDED WE FALL

Today is the day that Donald and Hailey were to celebrate their eleven-month anniversary. Instead, they were in an attorney's office finalizing separation papers. Saddened and angry, both parties felt that the other had failed them. Both individuals were upset because their new marriage did not work out. Instead of trying to overcome their obstacles, they both felt that since their initial investment wasn't that great, it would be easier to cut their losses and move on.

You have come to the Y in the road and have made the decision that your partner is crazy (I am lacking a better clinical term at the moment). You decide that it is early enough in the relationship for you to get out of it and take a loss for whatever you have invested and keep your life moving forward. Well, that is always a choice, a choice that many people take; hence, this is the number one reason for the high divorce rate that is ever increasing and is currently above a whopping 40%.

You get a divorce, sell the home or condo, move into an apartment and start all over. You blame the other person for the demise of the relationship because they had too many issues that they failed to disclose to you while you were dating. If you had known that person had so many problems, you would not have married him or her to begin with.

This line of thinking is normal, but faulty. When getting out of any relationship, the onus is on you to look at your role in the relationship and decide what you could have done differently. Once you have asked yourself this question, you can do some serious soul searching and began working on yourself. Or, you can continue to blame the other person and end up in relationship after relationship that is bound to fail because it is not the other person's issues. It is you, your stuff. Acknowledge it, own it, work on it, improve it and grow from it.

Ignoring one's issues reminds me of some soldiers doing field combat exercises when they don't want to be there. When they are practicing for a combat situation and are not in the mood to be there, it is very easy for a soldier to cop out and claim to not feel well in order to go to sick bay to avoid being in the line of fire in the midst of combat games. Simply stated, they do not want to put in the work. What have they left behind? They left people who depend on them – good, bad or indifferent – to fight it out no matter what the outcome.

The same will hold true for you in your relationship if you choose the road of walking away. The road to ending your relationship places you in a position where you have lost the battle before the war began. When you are faced with obstacles that you are not comfortable with, and it doesn't feel good because you are not able to take responsibility of your own issues, that road to ending those feelings sometimes looks pretty good.

Let's travel down that road for a minute. That road doesn't consist of the grass being greener; it is full of resentment, bitterness, inability to want to trust others again, and most of all, emptiness.

You married the person you are with for a reason. Do you remember why you married that person? You have some issues that have come to the surface that you did not expect or anticipate. Your partner has some issues and has come to some of the same conclusions. Now here you both are in the midst of being as vulnerable as you will ever be, and what will you do with that? This road leads people to expose the other person's issues and cast them as the villain. Not many people understand that you are supposed to go through this process in an effort to grow together and use this phase of vulnerability to trust each other on a level that allows your bond to be unbreakable.

Now, there are times in this phase in a relationship where I would say, "You need to move on. Count your blessings and be thankful that you were so quickly made aware of situations that would exacerbate as time goes on." Here are some of the issues in this early phase in your marriage that would be grounds to walk down the road to divorce – and do not look back!

EMOTIONAL ABUSE

Emotional abuse is described as any behavior intended to control and demean another person through the use of intimidation, fear, criticism, manipulation and many other tactics. These tactics can be effective in keeping the other person in the relationship and 'in their place.' The victim of this emotional control is internally suffering. This type of abuse deals a tremendous blow to an individual's self-esteem and well-being. If you are experiencing any form of this type of abuse, seek professional help. A professional counselor can assist you in deciding the right direction to go. There may be times that the abuser may not even understand that the tools they are using to get their needs met are detrimental to you as the spouse, and he or she may be willing to work on improving those behaviors through counseling. If you do not get help, these behaviors can intensify and lead to other expressions of abuse.

PHYSICAL ABUSE

Physical abuse is when an individual, whether a man or woman, actually causes harm to you by placing their hands on you to do damage.

Despite the images seen in the media, this is a cross-gender issue and can occur by either gender. Physical abuse is an issue of power and control and is intolerable in any situation. If you are experiencing any type of negative physical contact from your spouse/partner, call 9-1-1, and seek professional help immediately. There is an old saying that whatever your partner is doing that you don't like before you get married, only gets worse after the marriage. Physical abuse is not a situation that anyone can afford to have worsened. Please, seek professional help; you do not want to play with your life in the name of love.

In earlier chapters of this book, I spoke a great deal about keeping your family members out of your personal affairs with your spouse. Emotional and physical abuse situations are the exceptions to that rule. Tell someone, anyone and everyone, what is going on and try to get help to get out of that situation. You are deserving of someone to love you and treat you with respect and dignity. Love is never meant to hurt emotionally or physically to a level where you begin to not love yourself.

INFIDELITY

During this time of your life while you are indecisive about where you want your marriage to go, there can be individuals outside of your marriage that may seem to understand, and another relationship can develop during this process. I am not an advocate for any type of activity such as this, but I must address infidelity and, if faced with this issue, you will need to decide how you want to deal with it.

Again, instead of talking with your family and/or friends, seek professional help. Counseling will not only assist you in staying together, it will also empower you and allow you to develop the strength you will need to go through with any decision you make. As a therapist, I cannot, nor will not say that just because there has been infidelity in your marriage that you must leave. Life is not that simple, nor that easy. Look at our popular culture today where so many politicians have had public indiscretions and the spouses have chosen to stay in the relationship. The decision to stay is such an individual choice. Sure, people will judge you for your decision, but the decision is yours, and you must be willing to do the extra work of learning how to trust again if you choose to stay in the relationship.

At the end of the day, when all is said and done, we are all alone. The decisions you make are yours alone, so what will you decide? If after a tremendous amount of debate, deep thinking, prayer, and soul searching, you decide on a road to take, be comfortable and confident in your decision, whichever road you take. If you choose not to divide and go down the lonely road of divorce, then hold on tight, because being united is the other road to travel and I hope you have your seat belt on and are ready for the ride.

Questions to ask yourself when you have decided to walk away. Take time to answer the questions in this section.

1. What have you learned from this experience?

_____

_____

_____

_____

_____

2. What role did you play in this situation?

_____

_____

_____

_____

_____

3. What are you willing to do differently as you move forward?

_____

_____

_____

_____

_____

4. What issues didn't you address that led to your break up?

_____

_____

_____

_____

_____

5. What patterns were present in your lives that have brought you here to this moment?

_____

_____

_____

_____

_____

6. Where do you hope that this road will take you? Why?

_____

_____

_____

_____

_____

UNITED WE STAND

Tim and Julie were contemplating getting a divorce after six months of marriage. They sought counsel from their pastor in church and were able to work through many of their issues. Today, they have been married for six years and often talk about the time when they almost ended the best thing that ever happened to them.

No matter how indecisive you are – and it doesn't matter how long during your first year of marriage it takes for you to make a decision – you ultimately decide that you are worthy and you are committed to your partner, and you choose the road to stay together. You honor your vows, you honor your love. You are willing to face the pain, the hurts, the insecurities and the vulnerabilities that are now exposed. You are willing, no matter how difficult the situation is, to acknowledge your partner's quirks and support him or her in learning and growing so you can be a strong unit.

This chapter reminds me of being a little girl and fighting with my siblings. I was the oldest child, and my brother and sister were one year apart. They were inseparable; everyone thought they were twins. My sister was a tom-boy and everywhere my brother went, she followed right behind him. Where was I? I was always in some quiet corner reading a book while they were busy outside getting into some mischief. They would often come in the house with night crawlers, worms, or anything slimy and throw them on me. As long as they knew it could get my goat, they would do it. Their mischief always caused a battle. It was always me against them. Happily, it always ended up in laughter. But, no matter how much we fought as siblings, no other children in the neighborhood could taunt or try to hurt any of us. Why? Because when it really mattered, United We Stood!

Knowing that you must go through a period of teasing out your individual issues while learning how to deal with your partner's is a key component to getting through this Y in the road. It is going to be important that you understand your alliance should always be with your spouse, even though you are not getting along. No matter what, you may feel all alone in your efforts, but if your partner also shows commitment to the marriage, it is well worth the fight to be united in your journey.

You have chosen the road that will allow you to stay with your significant other. Now, what does this road have in store for you? There will be sunny days, cloudy days; there will be construction on the road that delays your progress. There will be a great many daily life issues that can bring your hard work to a complete halt. But as long as you are willing to drive down this road, and I would recommend doing so with professional assistance, you will eventually be able to address your issues, grow as a couple, and even take some time to get out of the car and smell the roses.

Questions to ask yourself as you have decided to stay together and work through your issues. Take time to answer the questions in this section.

1. What are you fighting for?

   _____

   _____

   _____

   _____

   _____

2. What have you learned about yourself during this process?

   _____

   _____

   _____

   _____

   _____

3. Have you decided to seek professional help to assist you with working through your issues? Why or why not?

   _____

   _____

   _____

   _____

   _____

4. What is your plan for utilizing different communication tools in the future and what are they?

_____

_____

_____

_____

_____

5. What are the three core issues you face as a couple that you believe are dividing you and how have you addressed them?

_____

_____

_____

_____

6. Discuss the strengths that you both possess that are keeping you together.

_____

_____

_____

_____

RULES OF ENGAGEMENT

After Archie and Victoria attended a couples' seminar to strengthen their union, they had much homework to complete. They had to develop the framework of what their blueprint of life should look like in order to have a foundation to build on. Although it was difficult, both Archie and Victoria were willing to ask questions and come up with answers that would work for their lives as a couple. Upon completing the hard work, they were able to come up with their rules of engagement.

After making your final decision at the Y in your road, I am hopeful that you have chosen the path that will allow you to stick it out in your marriage, work on your issues, learn to accept your partner's issues and grow together. I do not want to paint the picture that you will both grow at the same time and at the same pace. You must find the patience to allow your partner to grow in his or her own time and space and with your support, and vice versa.

In the chapter discussing The Catch, I talked about the couple developing their mission, and vision and purpose for their marriage. The marriage, as mentioned earlier is a legal, binding contract, and on a very basic level, the marriage should have the basic foundation of a business.

The marriage should have a mission, vision, and purpose. If you didn't develop those basic tenants in the earlier part of your relationship, now is the time to do so. In addition to having the necessary fundamentals to guide your relationship, the rules of engagement should now be developed. Since you have probably said some things that you regret or have made some key mistakes, you can now begin to develop rules to guide your relationship that will keep you honest and remind you of your foundational supports.

One of the rules that you would want to abide by is: not going to sleep angry with one another. Even if you do not have resolution about a disagreement, it is OK to say, "Tonight, we must agree to disagree, I love you, and I need you, and I would like to have more dialogue about this issue when we have had some time to think about the situation." Another rule is to always treat each other with respect. Speaking to each other from a place of respect and love is necessary to honor your partner's feelings.

I am excited to bring to the women who are reading this book a much-needed tool for improving communication from a place of respect. Women often prefer to discuss issues when the issue is at the forefront of their mind. In an effort to keep you from keeping your spouse on the defensive, please do not begin a conversation with the proverbial phrase, "Can we talk?" or "We need to talk". Those words automatically place your partner on the defensive, which makes it difficult for them to receive your message as they are very busy trying to figure out how to get out of the line of fire. If you were in a position where you were already having general, enjoyable conversation, and just haphazardly brought up your concerns in casual discussion, you would be amazed at the outcome of your conversation. This is a rule of engagement that you should practice on a consistent basis.

Throughout your relationship, each person can and may become interested in different social outlets such as enjoying different movies, music, friends and social activities. The key to keeping a lasting, loving relationship is to periodically have an interest review. People change! It doesn't mean that your partner doesn't want to be with you if their interests have changed. Most often, your partner would like to have your support in knowing that you are open to whatever they are experiencing in life. Each of you must have a clear understanding as to how you process and deal with change. Not only for this particular situation, but in all areas of your life.

The best recommendation that I can give you to ensure success in your marriage is to always, always take a step back when an argument is ensuing and ask yourself: "What is my expectation that didn't get met that is causing this conflict?" Once you have discovered your expectation, you are able to return to your partner and discuss the true issue and avoid many hurtful situations.

If you are following your basic rules of engagement, and keeping the three-strand cord in your forefront, then the second year of marriage and beyond will be a piece of cake. You have done all of the hard work now and have the tools to help you continue to get through issues as a unit. If you ever have a situation that seems to be too big to handle, contact a trusted neutral party such as a minister or a therapist to assist you with getting through your difficult time.

Congratulations for making it through your first year of marriage!

You have encountered a whirlwind of feelings, truths about yourself and your spouse. You have had to learn how to operate as a married person and not rely on the tools you used when you were single. You have learned to respect your spouse and give him or her permission to grow independently and to grow with you. You have loved each other like no other. You have created your foundation to build an empire like no other. You have become rich in knowledge through being vulnerable with each other. You have developed a spirituality to share together to help you through your hard times. You have learned the delicate balance of keeping your relatives out of your personal affairs while still being able to have a good relationship with them.

After all of the hard work you have completed, remember on your First Year Anniversary to enjoy the cake you put away from your union for this occasion. You deserve it!

Questions to ask yourself as you are developing your strategic plan for success. Take time to answer the questions in this section.

1. Review and discuss your mission, vision and purpose for this marriage.

   _____

   _____

   _____

   _____

   _____

2. What are your rules for dealing with conflict?

   _____

   _____

   _____

   _____

   _____

3. What issues are hot topics and how have you decided to address them as they come up in the future?

   _____

   _____

   _____

   _____

   _____

4. From your perspective, how could your core issues have been handled differently?

_____

_____

_____

_____

_____

5. How has this experience helped you grow as an individual and as a couple?

_____

_____

_____

_____

_____

6. How will you know when the rules need to change?

_____

_____

_____

_____

LET THE
MARRIAGE BEGIN!

Michael and Lauren were travelling across the country, driving their new Lexus. The couple took this opportunity to reflect on their trials and tribulations. They were able to discuss how they have grown as a couple. Finally, Lauren says to Michael, with a deep sigh, "After all that we have experienced in our first year of marriage, I now believe that we can finally let our marriage begin."

As a couple transitioning out of your first year of marriage, you will learn about your issues and how to begin to work on them. You will learn how not to impose your problems on your partner so that you do not have to address your own. You should have learned how to accept your partner's imperfections along with his or her strengths. There must be a fundamental understanding that what goes on within your relationship must stay there in order for your relationship to be successful. Keep family and friends out of your business! You have to learn that there is a give and take regarding mutual respect for one another. It is so important to be mindful of your words during the midst of a disagreement; always remember, you can apologize, but you can't take back the hurt.

The best aspect of the first year of marriage is the blissful love you should encounter. This is the best year because the love is fresh and you can't get enough of each other. Cherish these moments.

As you are moving toward your future together, keep in mind that you will always need to come to the table as a couple and evaluate your "family plan." Just as a business reviews its annual report, you will need to evaluate how you can improve and eliminate what is not working. You practice and perfect this skill by assessing the situation, identifying the issues, developing solutions to the issues, and implementing the solutions to resolve any problems you may incur. As a couple, you will need to reevaluate the new solutions you decided upon to find out if they work. If what you have implemented does not work, then by all means, you must go back to the drawing board and come up with another plan.

Up to now when getting married, there hasn't been a particular manual that comes along with the wedding gifts to help you through the process. This book should be considered your how-to manual to help you understand the phases that people do not realize exist. It allows you not to feel so alone in your journey, and most importantly, it allows you, if you do the work, to be successful in your marriage. So, now you are on the road to success and where you go from here is completely up to you. Enjoy the ride!

Questions to ask yourself when you have decided to stay together. Take time to answer the questions in this section.

1. What is the foundation on which your marriage is based?

_____

_____

_____

_____

_____

2. What had to change to induce growth in you and your spouse?

_____

_____

_____

_____

3. What will you need to continue to work on to keep the momentum going forward?

_____

_____

_____

_____

4. How will you know when you and your spouse need to review your "family plan?"

_____

_____

_____

_____

_____

5. What is the most important lesson you have learned from reading this book?

_____

_____

_____

_____

_____

6. Discuss how conflict in the marriage allowed you to grow individually.

_____

_____

_____

_____

Afterward

I wrote this book, and left it in my computer for quite some time before actually getting it published. I couldn't figure out why I didn't move on it when it was complete, but as fate would have it, I now realize that my journey was not yet finished. In having this book hibernate, life happened, and my life changed in so many ways. I currently live in a different city and with that change, amongst many others, I have met so many wonderful people along the way that God has strategically placed in my path to assist me with my journey to continuous growth and learning. So, I would like to give a special mention to all of these people for being so instrumental in my change/growth process, both personally and professionally. Each of you has been sent from God as a vessel of change and I am so grateful to have you in my life. To Sharon Scott, Carrie Johnson, Erica Clemmons-Manual, Eva Nelson-Brown, Ivonne Gonzalez Favela, Cassandra Jones, Colleen Jefferson, Trisha Thomas, Tiffany Glenn, Wendy Sellers, Cara Alexander and Momma Nancy, Belvia, Jean, Karla, Brenda, Rose, Stacy, Sophia, Helena, Kelly, Allison, Dawn, Sonya, Kimberly and Calvin Townsend and especially, Joseph Scott. Each of you has a special place in my heart, and I am thankful that you have been a part of my journey. I am hopeful that we have a chance to continue on the road to self-discovery and prosperity together.

ABOUT THE AUTHOR

Photo by J.Stearns
Beauty Beyond the Eye Photography

Delores "Gigi" Hamilton is a native of Toledo, Ohio. She holds a Bachelor of Arts degree from The University of Toledo and a Master of Arts degree from Bowling Green State University. Delores is a Licensed Professional Counselor, and Mental Wellness facilitator.

As a psychotherapist, she has worked with many couples who did not understand that work, adjusting and growing had to occur within the first year of marriage in order for the marriage to prosper and be successful. When obtaining the right tools for success, many couples were able to avoid many common pitfalls that occur within the first year of marriage that send so many people to divorce Court.

She says of *Let the Marriage Begin!*

"I created this book because of going through my first year of marriage and doing everything wrong. As I began counseling couples, I often noticed patterns that each couple would experience along with simple solutions to resolve them."

Delores offers counseling and retreats for couples. She also works with individuals to assist them with getting through difficult situations in their lives.

You can visit Delores "Gigi" Hamilton at
www.dreamworkspublishingpllc.com
and follow her on Twitter at
www.Twitter.com/DreamWorksPub

Reflection Journal

_____

_____

_____

_____

_____

_____

_____

_____

_____

_____

_____